Fact Finders®

PEOPLE YOU SHOULD KNOW

T0101146

MOHAMED SALAH

Get to Know the Soccer Superstar

by Nevien Shaabneh

Consultant: Dr. Saqib Qureshi
Football Coach and Armchair Pundit
Islamic Soccer League
Toronto, Canada

CAPSTONE PRESS
a capstone imprint

Fact Finders Books are published by Capstone Press
1710 Roe Crest Drive, North Mankato, Minnesota 56003
www.capstonepub.com

Library of Congress Cataloging-in-Publication Data
Names: Shaabneh, Nevien, author.
Title: Mohamed Salah : get to know the soccer superstar / by Nevien Shaabneh.
Description: North Mankato, Minnesota : Capstone Press, 2020. | Series: Fact
   finders. People you should know | Audience: Age 8–9. | Audience: K to
   Grade 3.
Identifiers: LCCN 2019005990| ISBN 9781543571851 (hardcover) | ISBN
   9781543574678 (paperback) | ISBN 9781543571929 (ebook pdf)
Subjects: LCSH: Salah, Mohamed, 1992– —Juvenile literature. | Soccer
   players—Egypt—Biography—Juvenile literature. | Soccer players—Great
   Britain—Biography—Juvenile literature.
Classification: LCC GV942.7.S195 S53 2020 | DDC 796.334092 [B] --dc23
LC record available at https://lccn.loc.gov/2019005990

Editorial Credits
Mari Bolte, editor; Kayla Rossow, designer; Tracy Cummins, media researcher;
Tori Abraham, production specialist

Photo Credits
Alamy: News Images/Alamy Live News, 27; Getty Images: Jan Kruger, 20, MOHAMED EL-SHAHED/AFP,
9; Newscom: CECIARINI FRANCESCA/SIPA, 16, Colin Lane/Mirrorpix, 7, 19, REUTERS/Albeiro Lopera,
12, REUTERS/GIAMPIERO SPOSITO, 23, REUTERS/Maarten Straetemans, 14, Simon Bellis/Sportimage, 5;
Shutterstock: Alizada Studios, Cover, eFesenko, 10, John Gomez, 24, lev radin, 29

Source Notes
page 8, line 9: James Carroll. "Mohamed Salah: in the Beginning . . . " https://www.liverpoolfc.com/news/first-team/283441-mohamed-salah-in-the-
beginning. Viewed 1 August, 2018.

page 10, line 9: Matt Porter. "'The Price For Him Was Very High and I'll Never Forget the Role He Played': Mohamed Salah Credits His Father For
Success as Liverpool Star Continues to Thrive at Anfield." https://www.dailymail.co.uk/sport/football/article-6504335/Mohamed-Salah-credits-
father-success-Liverpool.html. Viewed 13 August 2018.

page 12, line 4: Paulo Menicucci and Adrian Harte. "How Great Is Liverpool and Egypt's Mohamed Salah?" https://www.uefa.com/
uefachampionsleague/news/newsid=2528652.html. Viewed 2 August 2018.

page 15, line 1: James Carroll. "Mohamed Salah: Moving to Europe . . ." https://www.liverpoolfc.com/news/first-team/283444-mohamed-salah-
moving-to-europe. Viewed 2 August 2018.

page 17, line 13: Nizaar Kinsella. "Revealed: Why Liverpool Sensation Salah Failed at Chelsea." https://www.goal.com/en-us/news/revealed-the-
reason-why-liverpool-sensation-salah-failed-at/urc79is9135r1mvv2ydrxcxdr. Viewed 5 August 2018.

page 19, sidebar, line 10: Mark Brown. "Mo Salah Scores Again as Boots Enter British Museum Collection." https://www.theguardian.com/
football/2018/may/17/mo-salah-scores-boots-enter--british-museum-collection-liverpool-egypt. Viewed 20 September 2018.

page 22, line 8: CNN. "Mohamed Salah's Long Road to Stardom at Liverpool." https://www.youtube.com/watch?v=UhrlsnWLuQc. Viewed 12
September 2018.

page 22, line 11: Rory Smith. "Mo Salah of Liverpool Breaks Down Cultural Barriers, One Goal at a Time." https://www.nytimes.com/2018/05/02/
world/europe/mo-salah-liverpool-champions-league.html. Viewed 18 August 2018.

page 25, line 11: Jacque Talbot. "How Mohamed Salah Is Reshaping Britain's Perception of Islam." http://www.sportbible.com/football/football-how-
mohamed-salah-is-reshaping-britains-perception-of-islam-20180525. Viewed 26 July 2018.

page 28, line 14: Osha Mahmoud. "'Our Son': Mohamed Salah Splashes Cash to Give Home Village a Cleaner Future." https://www.middleeasteye.net/
news/Mohamed-Salah-Liverpool-Egypt-village. Viewed 28 July 2018.

All internet sites appearing in back matter were available and accurate when this book was sent to press.

TABLE OF CONTENTS

1

A SOCCER KING

Snow drizzles over a soccer pitch in mid-December 2017. It soaks the nets, the players, and the crowd. But the player in a red Premier League club Liverpool jersey marked with the number 11 doesn't seem to feel it. The end of the scoreless first half approaches.

Forward Mohamed Salah juggles the soccer ball on his right side. He hovers near the edge of the penalty area on the field. He blocks one player, who falls to the ground. He dodges another. Blue Everton jerseys surround him, but he plays as though no one else is there.

Mohamed curls the ball with his right foot before striking the ball with his left. An opponent tries to block it—he misses. The ball flies in the air. The goalkeeper makes a dramatic leap, but he can't get there in time. The ball hits the back of the net. Goal! The crowd cheers. Mohamed's teammates swarm him in a sea of red Liverpool jerseys, hugging him and patting him on the back.

Mohamed later said that the Everton score was his best goal with Liverpool.

Everton was able to score a goal in the second half, ending the game in a tie. But Mohamed's goal was seen by millions of soccer fans online. Their votes earned him the FIFA Puskás Award for best shot of the year. But it was only one of many awards he received during the 2017–2018 soccer season. He was named as one of the top 10 most valuable soccer players in the world. He also set a new Premier League record for the highest number of goals in a season by one player, at 32.

DID YOU KNOW?

The FIFA Puskás Award celebrates the best goal scored in a set 12-month period. Winners are chosen through an online vote. Mohamed's goal outscored overhead kicks by Real Madrid players Cristiano Ronaldo and Gareth Bale, along with seven other excellent shots.

Other Victories

Mohamed earned more than 30 honors in the 2017–2018 season. Some include:

- Premier League Player of the Month, which he earned three times

- Liverpool's Player of the Month, earned seven times

- Liverpool's Player of the Season

- Pro Footballers' Association (PFA) Player of the Month, earned four times

- PFA's Player of the Year

- Confederation of African Football's African Footballer of the Year

- BBC's African Footballer of the Year

Mohamed at the Liverpool Football Club Players' Awards in May 2018

2

A SUPERSTAR IS BORN

Mohamed Salah Ghaly was born in the small village of Nagrig, Egypt, on June 15, 1992. He came from a middle-class Muslim family. As a child, Mohamed found himself thinking more about soccer than his homework. He grew up passing the ball with his father and uncles, all soccer players. His favorite players were Francesco Totti, Ronaldo, and Zinédine Zidane. "I loved those kinds of players, players who played with magic," he said.

DID YOU KNOW?

Egypt's national football team is known as the Pharaohs. They are Africa's most successful team. They were the first team from a country not in Europe or the Americas to qualify for the World Cup.

the outside of Mohamed's family's house in Nagrig

Even when he was not physically running and kicking, he was watching soccer on TV or playing it on his PlayStation. He always picked Liverpool as his team.

When Mohamed was 14, the El Mokawloon El Arab Sporting Club visited the village. They came to watch another young player. But Mohamed captured their attention instead. He was invited to train with them.

The only problem was that the center was five hours away from his home. Mohamed had to make many sacrifices to attend the training. "I would complain that I didn't want to travel to training," he said later. "But [my father] stood by me and told me that all great players go through this. The price for him was very high, and I'll never forget the role he played in my career."

Cairo is home to nearly 20 million people.

Mohamed went to school from 7 a.m. to 9 a.m. Then he would walk more than a mile to a neighboring village to catch his first bus. Four more buses followed, until he finally reached Cairo around 2:30 p.m. After training for a few hours, he would repeat his journey in reverse. Most nights he was home by 10:30 p.m. This was his life, five days a week, for the next four years.

However, all his hard work and dedication was worth it when he made his professional **debut** with El Mokawloon in the Egyptian Premier League. He was 19 years old.

DID YOU KNOW?

Did you know that soccer is called football (pronounced fute-ball) outside of North America? American football is different from football in the rest of the world.

debut—a player's first game

3

ON THE MOVE

Mohamed was young to play nationally. Many professionals don't make their debut until their 20s. His speed and scoring ability were impressive. "He could compete in a race with [Olympic gold medal sprinter] Usain Bolt," a former coach bragged.

Mohamed (front row, left) played for Egypt during the FIFA U-20 World Cup in 2011. All players are under 20 years old.

The next year he represented Egypt at the 2012 Olympic Games in London, England. He scored a goal in three separate games. Egypt got to the quarterfinals for the first time since 1984. A loss to Japan knocked the team out of the tournament. Mohamed's performance earned him the nickname "The **Pharaoh**."

Mohamed's career continued to take off and soar to new heights. But his success did not come without **obstacles**. Just as Mohamed was set to play more championship league games for his Egyptian team, games were canceled.

The Riot

On February 1, 2012, the Egyptian soccer teams Al Masry and Al Ahly faced off in a match at the Port Said Stadium. Tensions between the clubs had always been high. After the match, Al Masry fans ran onto the field and attacked Al Ahly fans. Because the stadium doors were locked from the outside, people couldn't escape. In the end, 74 people were killed and another 500 were injured. League games were canceled for the next two years, and some pro players retired.

obstacle—something that gets in the way or prevents someone from doing something
pharaoh—a king of ancient Egypt

Just before the Olympics, Mohamed had signed a four-year contract with FC Basel, a Swiss football club. They had seen him in March when the club played the Pharaohs in a friendly match. It was a great opportunity. But it also meant Mohamed would have to move to Europe.

Mohamed takes shots primarily with his left foot but plays right wing.

"I grew up in Egypt, I knew everything in Egypt . . . but I didn't know anything in Switzerland," he said. "I couldn't understand any language because I couldn't speak English or Swiss German. . . . I went there and lived alone. It was a very difficult time because I didn't know what to do." He couldn't watch TV because there were no Egyptian channels. And because he was new and young, he was used as a substitute player. But he quickly improved. He made 47 appearances on the team, scoring nine goals. He helped Basel win the Swiss Super League's championship title during its 2012–2013 season.

DID YOU KNOW?

Soccer leagues are groups of teams, or clubs, that compete against another group of teams. The Egyptian Premier League is a professional league made up of 18 teams. The Pharaohs are one team. FC Basel is part of the Swiss Super League, which has 10 teams. Many teams have Football Club (FC) as part of their names.

Mohamed returned to Egypt to marry his fiancé, Magi, in 2013. His parents invited the entire village to the wedding. Thousands of people showed up to celebrate. A year later, Mohamed and Magi had a daughter they named Makka.

Mohamed playing in a Chelsea game against Stoke City in 2014

In 2014 Mohamed signed an £11 million deal with Chelsea FC. Chelsea plays in the Premier League, the highest level of English soccer. He played for Chelsea for 12 months, making just 19 appearances. It was a disappointing move.

The next year, Chelsea loaned Mohamed to Fiorentina, an Italian club in Tuscany, Italy, for four months. He flourished, scoring four **assists** and nine goals in the 26 games he played with the team. When the season ended, he signed with Roma, a club in Rome, Italy. He played there for two years, scoring 29 goals in 65 appearances. He used this time to grow as a player. "He improved during his spell at Italy, became more mature and improved physically," a former Chelsea coach observed.

DID YOU KNOW?

The Premier League is the most-watched league on Earth, having been created out of the English Division One. Matches are watched in more than 900 million homes across 190 countries. The six teams that have been in the league since it was founded in 1992 are Arsenal, Chelsea, Everton, Liverpool, Manchester United, and Tottenham Hotspur.

assist—a pass that leads to a goal by a teammate

BREAKING RECORDS

4

Mohamed's childhood dream came true in mid-2017. Liverpool paid a record £44 million for his contract. It was then the most expensive signing in Liverpool's history. Still, critics said Roma should have held out for more money before letting him out of his contract.

Mohamed scored nine goals in his first 12 Premier League games. This broke the previous record of eight goals by Robbie Fowler in 1993. Mohamed was the first Egyptian to win the Premier League's Player of the Month. He also became the first Premier League player to score 20 goals in all competitions in that season. He shares a record with World Cup winner Roger Hunt, who scored 23 goals before the New Year in 1961. It took 56 years for someone to match that record, but Mohamed did it.

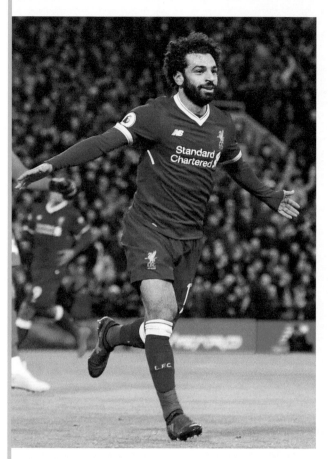

Mohamed's 2017–2018 year with Liverpool was a record-breaking season.

On Display

Before the Champions League final in 2018 the British Museum displayed a pair of Mohamed's boots alongside ancient Egyptian items. He wore the boots during his record-setting 32 league goals in the 2017–2018 season. "The boots tell a story of a modern Egyptian icon," the museum's keeper said.

DID YOU KNOW?

Mohamed was the first Egyptian player to sign with Liverpool.

Liverpool suited Mohamed. He began surpassing team records. By the end of January 2018, he had become the third-fastest player to score 25 goals in England's top flight league. The fastest and second-fastest records had been set in 1915 and 1996. In May he set the record for the most goals in a 38-game Premier League season. In October he became the fastest-ever player to score 50 goals, doing it in just 65 appearances.

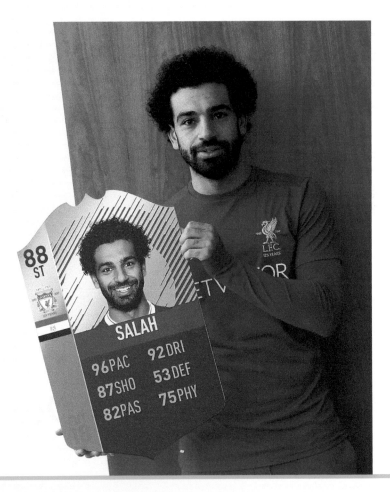

Mohamed was the first player to earn the EA Player of the Month award three times in one season.

In 2017 he helped the Pharaohs reach the World Cup Finals. They had qualified only twice before, in 1934 and 1990. The team competed in Russia in June 2018. Mohamed scored twice, matching the record for World Cup goals scored by an African player. Abdulrahman Fawzi set the previous record in 1934. Altogether, Mohamed broke close to 10 different records and won more than 30 awards through the end of 2018.

The Pharaohs played against Uruguay, Russia, and Saudi Arabia. Mohamed missed the first game because of a shoulder injury. He did what he could in the remaining two games, but in the end Egypt lost all three of their matches.

DID YOU KNOW?

More than 1 million voters wrote in Mohamed Salah's name during the Egyptian presidential election in 2018.

5 RITUALS ON AND OFF THE FIELD

When players score goals, some jump, some dance, and some cheer. Mohamed Salah has his own special **ritual**. After he celebrates with his teammates, he kneels down and bows his head toward the ground. Muslims call this act *sujood*. Although it puts a person in a low position, physically, it is seen as a high spiritual act. "It's like praying, or thanking God for what I have received," Mohamed explained. "I've always done that since I was young."

"He is someone who embodies **Islam**'s values and wears his faith on his sleeve," a representative from the Muslim Council of Britain said. "He has a likeability. He is the hero of the team. Liverpool, in particular, has rallied around him in a really positive way."

Mohamed is the only Premier League player to openly perform sujood on the soccer field.

DID YOU KNOW?

Liverpool fans have a chant supporting Mohamed. "Mo Salah-la-la-la-a/Mo Salah-la-la-la-a/If he's good enough for you, he's good enough for me/If he scores another few, then I'll be Muslim too/If he's good enough for you, he's good enough for me/Sitting in the mosque, that's where I wanna be."

Islam—the religion of Muslims, based on the teachings of the prophet Muhammad

ritual—an action that is always performed in the same way

23

There are 1.6 billion Muslims around the world. That's about 23 percent of the global population.

Mohamed isn't the first or only Muslim soccer star. But, as many news sources point out, he is the world's most visible one. He posts about his faith on social media. His wife dresses modestly and wears a veil. Their daughter, Makka, is named after the holy city of Mecca. His beard, thick accent, and open demonstration of his religion remind fans of his Arab heritage.

Some people **discriminate** against immigrants or those of different faiths. Mohamed and other Muslim players have been harassed or threatened, both on and off the soccer field. Some people have even called for Muslims to be detained or **deported** from the United Kingdom. Discrimination in soccer rose by nearly 60 percent from 2017 to 2018. However, Mohamed's presence on the soccer pitch has changed some of that.

"He is an absolute positive role model for the Muslim and non-Muslim community here in the UK and around the world," a leader at Liverpool's Abdullah Quilliam Mosque said. "He has changed the perception of some of the negative beliefs that people have about the Islamic faith." In April 2018 Mohamed was given a piece of land in Mecca. The reward was, in part, because of Mohamed's positive representation of Islam in the United Kingdom.

deport—to force people to go back to their country of origin
discriminate—to treat people unfairly because of their race, country of birth, or gender

6 THE HAPPINESS MAKER

Mohamed is not only known as a soccer star. He is also a **philanthropist** who cares about his hometown of Nagrig. After Mohamed helped earn Egypt a World Cup spot in 2017, it was rumored that a businessman offered him a fancy house. Instead, Mohamed asked the businessman to make a donation to his village.

He still thinks of Nagrig as home. He and his wife honeymooned there. He returns during **Ramadan** every year, visiting local shops and signing autographs for anyone who wants one. Three cafés have opened in the village so local fans can watch the games.

The people of Nagrig call Mohamed "The Happiness Maker." The children of the village can now practice soccer in a new sports center. There is new hospital equipment, an ambulance unit, and a renovated school. About 400 families in the village receive assistance from the Salah Foundation. He has built a gymnasium, bought hospital equipment, rebuilt schools, and supplied an ambulance.

Liverpool fans have several songs they sing for Mohamed. His favorite is one called "Egyptian King."

philanthropist—a person who gives time or money to help others
Ramadan—the holy month of the Islamic calendar; Muslims fast from sunrise to sunset during Ramadan

Through hard work and talent, Mohamed Salah has risen to a high level of stardom. But his down-to-earth personality, his modesty, and his desire to help others makes this larger-than-life star admirable too. He visits his hometown often. He still loves the Egyptian national dish called koshary, a carb-heavy mixture of Egyptian spices, rice, pasta, lentils, onions, tomato sauce, and chickpeas. He speaks up for women's rights and lends his voice to anti-drug campaigns. And he continues to succeed on the soccer field.

During an acceptance speech, Mohamed said, "I want to dedicate this award to all the kids in Africa and Egypt. I want to tell them to never stop dreaming, never stop believing."

Mohamed starred in videos for a drug addiction campaign in Egypt. They were watched more than 8 million times in the first 3 days.

Make A Wish

In 2018 the Liverpool team visited the United States. Sixteen-year-old Ammar, a Syrian refugee with muscular dystrophy, asked the Make-A-Wish Foundation for the chance to meet Mohamed. The soccer star granted the wish, visiting Ammar and his family.

GLOSSARY

assist (uh-SIST)—a pass that leads to a goal by a teammate

debut (DAY-byoo)—a player's first game

deport (di-PORT)—to force people to go back to their country of origin

discriminate (dis-KRI-muh-nayt)—to treat people unfairly because of their race, country of birth, or gender

Islam (ISS-luhm)—the religion of Muslims, based on the teachings of the prophet Muhammad

obstacle (OB-stuh-kuhl)—something that gets in the way or prevents someone from doing something

pharaoh (FAIR-oh)—a king of ancient Egypt

philanthropist (fuh-LAN-throh-pist)—a person who gives time or money to help others

Ramadan (RAHM-i-dahn)—the holy month of the Islamic calendar; Muslims fast from sunrise to sunset during Ramadan

ritual (RICH-oo-uhl)—an action that is always performed in the same way

READ MORE

Battista, Brianna. *Cristiano Ronaldo*. New York: PowerKids Press, 2019.

Fishman, Jon M. *Soccer's G.O.A.T.: Pele, Lionel Messi, and More.* Minneapolis: Lerner Publications, 2020.

Wilson, Paula M. *Liverpool F.C.* New York: Av2 by Weigl, 2018.

INTERNET SITES

Liverpool F.C.
https://www.liverpoolfc.com/welcome-to-liverpool-fc

Olympic Games: Soccer
https://www.olympic.org/football

Premier League
https://www.premierleague.com/

CRITICAL THINKING QUESTIONS

1. What are some habits or characteristics that Mohamed showed as a young boy that might have helped him succeed?

2. What are some difficulties Mohamed had to face as a professional soccer player?

3. In what ways has Mohamed used his fame as a soccer player to help others?

INDEX